tartares &
Carpaccios

Recipes by Marie-Victoire Garcia
Photography by Akiko Ida

HACHETTE
Illustrated

contents

CARPACCIOS

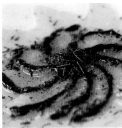

tips and tricks

Raw food: new taste sensations

The passion for natural things has reached our tables.

Nowadays, refrigeration and preserving techniques, which ensure correct temperatures and compulsory health controls, mean that raw meat and fish can be eaten safely.

Preparing a dish of raw ingredients sometimes means simply decorating it, touch by touch as a painter might. The result is a feast for your guests' eyes matching that for their palates as they discover new textures and flavours.

One word of advice: tartares and carpaccios should not be prepared several hours in advance of serving but eaten immediately.

You can, however, take time for an aperitif … accompanied by a carpaccio or tartare canapé.

Tartare

Most of us have heard of, or even seen, the traditional plate of raw red meat decorated with an egg yolk and accompanied by a variety of condiments.

Modern tartares have a new take, using a wide range of white meats, fish, shellfish, fruit or vegetables.

Everything is still raw, cut in little cubes or chopped, and finely seasoned to enhance the special taste of each ingredient.

Carpaccio

This dish comes to us from Italy.

There is a story of the Venetian chef who served a countess (on a diet) with a plate of raw beef fillet sliced very finely. Her guests remarked on the dish's resemblance to a work by the celebrated local painter, Carpaccio.

Nowadays, carpaccio means a dish made using paper-thin slices of meat, fish and, latterly, vegetables or fruit, all sprinkled at the last minute with a fruity oil.

The techniques

Absolutely fresh ingredients

Tartares and carpaccios have one thing
in common: the ingredients must be
cold and fresh, especially meat, fish
and shellfish.

Make sure, therefore, to alert your
butcher or fishmonger that you intend
to serve your purchases raw.

A final cold spell

Meat and fish will be easier to cut if
left for some time in the refrigerator
or the freezer, to firm up the flesh.
The chilling time depends on the dish
to be served.

A trick for carpaccio

Brush the slices of meat or fish carefully
with a little oil so that they do not stick
together.

Utensils

A mandoline

Fruit and vegetables can be sliced very
rapidly and uniformly with the help of an
adjustable mandoline, or one of the new
microplane graters and shavers.

A long-bladed knife

It goes without saying that an electric
knife will enable you to carve very fine
carpaccios. If you do not have one, a
well-sharpened long-bladed knife, will
do the trick for tartares and carpaccios.
Never use a saw-toothed knife.

A swivel-blade vegetable peeler

For some vegetables (such as shaving
carrots or cucumber in long strips), you
will find this type of vegetable peeler so
marvellous that you will not want to do
without it.

Warning

This book contains dishes that are
made with raw or lightly cooked eggs.
These should be avoided by vulnerable
people such as pregnant and nursing
mothers, invalids, the elderly, babies
and young children.

Beef tartare

Serves 4

500 g (1 lb) beef fillet, minced on the day of serving

1 large white onion, chopped

2 teaspoons strong mustard

1 teaspoon Worcestershire sauce

3 tablespoons ketchup

1 teaspoon wine vinegar

2 tablespoons olive oil

4 egg yolks, each in a half shell

salt and freshly ground black pepper

Chill the beef in the refrigerator for 15 minutes.

Mix together all the ingredients for the dressing.

Add the well-chilled beef and mix in well, allowing plenty of air to get into the blend. Divide into 4 portions and shape each into a mound. Place one mound on each plate and make a small indentation in the top to house the egg yolk in its half-shell. Serve immediately.

Suggestion

You could make a more exotic Asian-style tartare by adding a garnish of chopped coriander leaves and/or sesame seeds.

Spiced veal tartare

Serves 4

400 g (14 oz) veal fillet

2 teaspoons mustard

¼ teaspoon freshly ground black pepper

¼ teaspoon Cayenne pepper

2 tablespoons lemon juice

2 tablespoons olive oil

2 teaspoons Cognac

6 tablespoons chopped flat-leaf parsley

2 tablespoons snipped chives

2 tablespoons crème fraîche

salt

Refrigerate the veal fillet for an hour to firm it, then cut into very small cubes.

In a bowl mix together the mustard, pepper, Cayenne pepper, lemon juice, olive oil and Cognac. Season with salt to taste.

Add the parsley and chives and mix in well.

Add the contents of the bowl to the veal and stir in well, raising the mixture to aerate it.

Divide the tartare into four portions. Put neatly onto 4 plates and add a dollop of crème fraîche to each.

Suggestions

If serving this tartare as a starter, arrange it on a bed of grated carrots or serve with other crudités.

If served as a main dish, it goes very well with sautéed potatoes.

Salmon and coriander tartare

Serves 4

500 g (1 lb) fresh salmon fillet

4 tablespoons lemon juice

2 tablespoons olive oil

1 tablespoon wine or raspberry vinegar

3 tablespoons coriander leaves

salt and freshly ground black pepper

4 small ramekins

Freeze the salmon for 30 minutes to firm the flesh.

Slice as finely as possible.

Mix together the lemon juice, olive oil, vinegar and coriander leaves, reserving a few leaves for a garnish.

Add the sliced salmon to this mixture.

Divide into 4 and put into the ramekins.

To serve, turn out each ramekin onto a plate and garnish with the remaining coriander leaves.

Suggestion

Chives or fresh dill leaves could be substituted for the coriander.

Mackerel and chive tartare

Serves 4

4 smoked, peppered mackerel fillets (sold vacuum-packed)

6 tablespoons lemon juice

300 g (10 fl oz) plain or Greek yogurt

1 bunch of chives, snipped

Remove the mackerel skin and cut the fillets into very small pieces with a knife or, better, with sharp kitchen scissors.

Flatten the pieces with the back of a spoon.

Mix the lemon juice in a bowl with the yogurt and chives then add the mackerel.

Refrigerate until ready to serve.

Suggestion

This mackerel tartare makes a good starter served on slices of toasted baguette.

Marinated herring tartare

Serves 4

6 herring fillets (sold vacuum-packed)

2 onions, finely chopped

225 ml (8 fl oz) crème fraîche

1 large crisp dessert apple (organic, if possible, to use the skin)

Chop the herring fillets finely (lengthways or in squares).

Mix with the chopped onions and add the crème fraîche.

Just before serving, grate the unpeeled apple and add it to the mixture.

When the apple has been added, this tartare will keep in the refrigerator until the following day.

Serve on toast.

Variation (see photograph)

The herring fillets could also be cut into strips and formed into rounds. Then add a dollop of crème fraîche and top with the finely chopped apple and chopped onion.

Mixed vegetable tartare

Serves 4

2 firm tomatoes

2 small courgettes

1 small cucumber

3 carrots

10 pink radishes

5 small cauliflower florets

5 small broccoli florets

1 stick celery

1 spring onion

For the dressing:

4 tablespoons lemon juice

1 teaspoon strong mustard

1 teaspoon Worcestershire sauce

150 g (5 fl oz) natural yogurt

salt and freshly ground black pepper

4 small ramekins

Wash and dry all the vegetables carefully.

Dice them as finely as possible with a well-sharpened knife. (Leave the skin on the tomatoes, courgettes and cucumber).

Mix together the diced vegetables in a salad bowl.

Mix together the dressing ingredients and pour over the vegetables.

Mix again and put into the ramekins. Refrigerate for 15 minutes. Turn out each ramekin onto a plate before serving.

Variation

Any kinds of vegetables can be used for this tartare. Season with fresh herbs according to the vegetables you choose.

Tomato, feta cheese and basil tartare

Serves 4

500 g (1 lb) cherry tomatoes

200 g (7 oz) feta cheese, finely diced

1 tablespoon olive oil

1 bunch of basil

salt

4 small ramekins

Wash and deseed the cherry tomatoes. Cut in small pieces and divide among the ramekins.

Mix the olive oil and feta then add half the basil leaves. Feta is a salty cheese so check for taste before seasoning with salt.

Pour over the tomatoes and mix well.

Divide the mixture between the ramekins and decorate with the remaining basil leaves before serving.

Suggestion

The feta could be replaced by ricotta or mozzarella.

Cucumber and dill tartare

Serves 4

2 cucumbers (organic if possible) unpeeled

1½ tablespoons white wine vinegar

2 shallots, finely chopped

6 tablespoons olive oil

4 artichoke hearts

2 firm tomatoes, deseeded

8 dill sprigs

salt and freshly ground black pepper

Wash and dry the cucumbers.

Using a mandoline, slice one of the cucumbers into very fine rounds. Put in a colander, sprinkle with salt and leave to drain for 20 minutes.

Quarter the second cucumber lengthways. Remove the central core with the seeds and finely dice the rest.

Place in another colander, sprinkle with salt and leave to drain for 20 minutes.

To make the dressing, mix together the vinegar, shallots and the olive oil in a bowl. Season with salt and pepper.

Arrange the cucumber slices on plates in overlapping circles. Place an artichoke heart in the middle of each plate and pour over a teaspoon of the dressing.

Finely chop the tomatoes and mix with the diced cucumber . Garnish each artichoke with the mixture.

Just before serving, pour the remaining dressing over each plate and sprinkle with chopped dill.

Tartare of artichoke with tarragon

Serves 4

4 artichoke hearts

4 palm hearts

400 g (14 oz) mozzarella cheese

4 firm tomatoes

4 tablespoons olive oil

½ bunch tarragon

salt

4 small ramekins

Finely dice the artichoke hearts, palm hearts and mozzarella and mix together thoroughly in a bowl.

Deseed the tomatoes and dice finely. Add to the bowl.

Mix together the olive oil, tarragon leaves and salt to taste. Add to the bowl and mix well.

Divide the mixture among the ramekins, packing them firmly, then refrigerate for 15 minutes.

Just before serving, turn out onto 4 plates.

Suggestion

Basil can be used instead of tarragon, if you prefer. It also goes very well with mozzarella and tomato.

Tartare of minted peaches and pears

Serves 4

1 ripe white peach

3 tablespoons light brown soft sugar

a few mint leaves, chopped

2 tablespoons lemon juice

3 firm pears

2 firm yellow peaches

12 raspberries

4 small ramekins

Peel the white peach and purée it with the sugar and the chopped mint leaves.

Pour the lemon juice over the mixture immediately.

Peel the pears and the yellow peaches and cut them into small pieces.

Pour the white peach and mint purée over the pears and yellow peaches and mix well.

Divide among the ramekins, pack down firmly, cover with clingfilm and refrigerate until ready to serve.

To serve, turn out each ramekin onto a plate and decorate with sprigs of mint and a few raspberries.

Tartare of pineapple and mangoes with coconut milk

Serves 4

1 pineapple

4 mangoes

vanilla sugar or icing sugar, for dusting

200 ml (7 fl oz) coconut milk

coconut flakes, to decorate

Cut off the top and bottom of the pineapple and remove the skin.

Cut four large rounds from the middle of the pineapple and put one on each plate.

Finely dice the rest of the pineapple.

Cut the mangoes in half, running a knife around the nut to remove it. Take off the skin and finely dice the flesh.

Scatter the diced mango around each pineapple slice, reserving the equivalent of one mango.

Mix together the remaining diced pineapple and mango and spoon onto the centre of each pineapple round.

Dust each plate with vanilla sugar or icing sugar and sprinkle lightly with coconut milk.

Decorate with flaked coconut. Serve immediately.

Tartare of strawberries with basil

Serves 4

50 g (2 oz) pine nuts

500 g (1 lb) strawberries

½ dessert apple

2 tablespoons lemon juice

8 basil leaves, plus 1 or 2 to decorate each ramekin

4 tablespoons olive oil

1½ tablespoons caster sugar

zest of one unwaxed, or well-scrubbed lemon

Lightly toast the pine nuts in a pan, turning constantly.

Wash the strawberries and cut into small pieces.

Peel the half-apple and cut into small dice. Sprinkle over the lemon juice immediately, to prevent it discolouring.

Put the basil leaves, pine nuts, olive oil and sugar in a blender and process briefly.

Remove to a bowl. Add the strawberries and diced apple and stir gently.

Divide the mixture into ramekins, glasses or plates. Decorate with basil leaves and the lemon zest.

Suggestion

You could also decorate with red berries such as redcurrants or raspberries.

Beef carpaccio

Serves 4

400 g (14 oz) fillet of beef

4 tablespoons fruity olive oil

2 tablespoons lemon juice

60 g (2 oz) Parmesan cheese

4 basil sprigs

salt and freshly ground black pepper

For the pear variation

2 pears, peeled and sliced

For the marinade:

juice of 1/2 orange

1 stick cinnamon

2 teaspoons light brown soft sugar

1/4 teaspoon cumin seeds

1/4 teaspoon pink peppercorns

1/4 teaspoon crushed cardamom seeds

zest of 1/4 lemon

Wrap the fillet of beef in clingfilm and freeze for 1 hour then unwrap and slice very finely with a well-sharpened knife. If the slices are not fine enough, put them between two pieces of clingfilm and flatten gently with a rolling pin.

Arrange the slices on well-chilled plates.

Mix together the oil and lemon juice and brush over the strips of beef. Cover the plates with clingfilm and refrigerate for 20 minutes.

Finely shave the Parmesan. When ready to serve, season the carpaccio with salt and pepper to taste and add the Parmesan shavings.

Pour over the remaining oil and lemon juice and decorate with basil leaves.

Variation with pears (see photograph)

While the beef is resting in the freezer, mix together the ingredients for the pear marinade and steep the sliced pears in it.

Proceed as for the classic carpaccio up to the point when you take the plates from the refrigerator. Season the carpaccio and drizzle over the oil and lemon mixture.

Drain the pear slices and arrange between the slices of beef. Garnish with the lemon zest.

Serve immediately.

Carpaccio of duck with oranges

Serves 4

4 small oranges (preferably organic)

2 smoked duck breasts

juice of ½ orange

2 tablespoons lemon juice

1 teaspoon runny honey

1 teaspoon French mustard

4 tablespoons olive oil

1 teaspoon coriander seeds

1 teaspoon pink peppercorns

4 tarragon sprigs, to garnish

fleur de sel **or fine sea salt, freshly ground black pepper**

Wash, dry, and finely slice the oranges. Arrange the slices on 4 plates.

Cut the duck into very fine slices, carefully removing any traces of fat. Arrange the slices in a fan shape on the plates.

Mix together the orange and lemon juice, honey, mustard and olive oil and brush over the slices of duck. Trickle the remaining mixture around the plates.

Sprinkle with coriander seeds, pink peppercorns, salt and pepper. Garnish with the tarragon sprigs.

Chill the plates in the refrigerator for 20 minutes before serving.

Veal carpaccio

Serves 4

400 g (14 oz) fillet of veal

4 tablespoons olive oil

2 cloves garlic, crushed

1 teaspoon coriander seeds, cracked

1 teaspoon oregano

salt and freshly ground pepper

For the tuna variation

100 g (3½ oz) tuna, canned in oil

Put the veal fillet in the freezer for 45 minutes.

At the same time, chill 4 plates in the refrigerator (for around 30 minutes).

Slice the veal fillets very finely and arrange on the cold plates. Brush with olive oil.

Sprinkle the meat with the crushed garlic, coriander seeds and oregano.

Drizzle the remaining olive oil over each plate. Season to taste and serve immediately.

Variation with tuna

Scatter tuna flakes over the veal slices and continue as above.

Carpaccio of prawns with coriander and dill

Serves 4

12 gambas (large prawns), very fresh

zest of 1 unwaxed, or well-scrubbed, lemon

4–5 coriander sprigs, snipped

4–5 dill sprigs, snipped

juice of 2 limes

4 tablespoons olive oil

80 g (3 oz) Parmesan cheese, crumbled

salt and freshly ground black pepper

Peel the prawns and cut them in half along their length. Take out the black 'vein'.

Put the prawn halves on 4 plates. Sprinkle them with the lemon zest, coriander and dill.

Chill the plates in the refrigerator for 30 minutes.

When ready to serve, pour over the lime juice and olive oil. Season, then sprinkle with the crumbled Parmesan.

Salmon carpaccio with ginger and lime

Serves 4

400 g (14 oz) salmon fillet
or steak, skinned and
boned

2–4 cm (1–2 inches) fresh
ginger, grated

juice of 2 limes

4 tablespoons olive oil

5 tablespoons light soy
sauce (to serve)

salt

Freeze the salmon for 30 minutes to firm up the flesh.

Cut it into very fine slices and arrange on 4 plates.

Sprinkle with the grated ginger to taste, then pour over the lime juice and olive oil. Season to taste with salt.

Hand round the soy sauce separately.

Suggestion

Although the salmon is not served as sushi, the dressing used means it will go very well with rice, served with slices of baguette.

Tuna carpaccio with capers

Serves 4

400 g (14 oz) fresh tuna

3 tablespoons capers

1 bunch of flat-leaf parsley, snipped

zest of ½ unwaxed, or well-scrubbed, lemon

8 tablespoons of lemon juice

5 tablespoons olive oil

salt and freshly ground pepper

Freeze the tuna for 30 minutes to firm the flesh.

When ready, cut it in very fine strips with a well-sharpened knife and arrange on 4 plates.

Sprinkle over the capers, parsley and lemon zest. Pour over the lemon juice to taste.

Chill the plates in the refrigerator for 30 minutes.

When ready to serve, season with salt and pepper and drizzle a little olive oil over each plate.

Suggestion

Arrange the tuna strips on a bed of oak-leaf lettuce.

Carpaccio of salmon with lemon

Serves 4

400 g (14 oz) salmon fillet

juice of 1 lemon

5 teaspoons olive oil

2 teaspoons soy sauce

50 g (2 oz) pine nuts

50 g (2 oz) Parmesan
cheese shavings

150 g (5 oz) mesclun or
salad leaves

20 basil leaves, to garnish

salt and freshly ground
black pepper

For the mushroom variation

300 g (10 oz) button
mushrooms

juice of 1 lime

4 tablespoons crème
fraîche

12 chive stalks, snipped

Freeze the salmon fillet for 30 minutes to firm the flesh.

Cut into very fine slices and arrange on 4 plates.

Mix together the lemon juice, olive oil and soy sauce and pour over the salmon. Chill the plates in the refrigerator for 30 minutes.

Dry-fry the pine nuts in a non-stick pan, stirring constantly.

Sprinkle the plates with Parmesan shavings and toasted pine nuts.

Surround with the mesclun or salad leaves. Season with salt and pepper to taste, garnish with basil leaves and serve immediately.

Variation with mushrooms

Slice the mushrooms and sprinkle them with lime juice.

Take the salmon carpaccio from the refrigerator, where it has been macerating in its dressing, and add the mushroom slices to the plates.

Add a tablespoon of crème fraîche to each serving. Scatter over the chopped chives and Parmesan shavings.

Suggestion

This salmon carpaccio can be served as a substantial starter but you can easily turn it into a main dish by adding green vegetables or rice.

Carpaccio of scallops with chives

Serves 4

16 scallops

juice of 1 lime

4 tablespoons olive oil

1 teaspoon pink peppercorns

1 tablespoon snipped chives

¼ small red pepper, chopped

***fleur de sel* or fine sea salt**

Freeze the scallops for 10 minutes to firm them.

Remove the roe (the orange part) if necessary and slice each scallop into fine strips.

Arrange them on the plates.

Mix together the dressing ingredients and pour over the scallops and around each dish. Serve immediately.

Suggestions

If you find lime juice a bit too sharp, you can substitute lemon juice.

A finely chopped shallot will enhance the flavour of this maritime dish.

Carpaccio of sea bass with fennel

Serves 4

600 g (1 1/4 lb) fillet of sea bass

4 tablespoons lemon juice

5 tablespoons olive oil

1/4 teaspoon dill seeds

1 clove garlic, crushed

1 tablespoon white wine

1 teaspoon white sugar

1 small fennel bulb

salt and white pepper

Wrap the sea bass in clingfilm and freeze for 30 minutes.

Mix together the lemon juice, olive oil, dill seeds, garlic, white wine and sugar. Season with salt and pepper to taste.

Remove the fish from the freezer and cut it into very thin slices. Arrange them on 4 plates.

Slice the fennel bulb into small pieces and arrange on the plates. Scatter the fennel leaves over the fish.

When ready to serve, pour the dressing mixture over the fish.

Suggestion

If fresh dill is available, use it instead of dill seeds.
Crushed aniseed also goes well with fennel.

Carpaccio of courgettes with toasted pine nuts

Serves 4

2 courgettes

50 g (2 oz) pine nuts

4 tablespoons lemon juice

50 g (2 oz) Parmesan cheese

3 tablespoons olive oil

salt and freshly ground pepper

Slice the courgettes into very thin rounds with a mandoline set on the finest blade. Arrange the slices on plates.

Dry-fry the pine nuts in a non-stick pan, turning constantly. Scatter them over the courgettes.

Sprinkle the lemon juice over and chill the plates in the refrigerator for 30 minutes.

When ready to serve, shave the Parmesan into flakes; season the courgettes with salt and pepper to taste and pour over the olive oil. Scatter over the Parmesan shavings.

Suggestions

Several snippets of chives added with the lemon juice will enhance the flavour of this dish.

For those who like it, garlic can also be added.

Carpaccio of mushrooms

Serves 4

600 g (1¼ lb) button mushrooms

8 tablespoons of lemon juice

1 tablespoon balsamic vinegar

3 tablespoons olive oil

2 cloves garlic, chopped

2 tablespoons chopped parsley

salt and freshly ground pepper

Wipe the mushrooms. Remove the stalks, which can be used in another recipe, such as a salad.

Slice the mushrooms very finely with a knife, or a mandoline if you have one.

Arrange the slices on plates and immediately pour over half of the lemon juice, to keep them from discolouring.

Mix together the balsamic vinegar, olive oil, remaining lemon juice to taste, the chopped garlic and parsley.

Season with salt and pepper to taste and pour the vinaigrette over the carpaccio. Serve immediately.

Suggestion

This carpaccio makes a good starter.

Carpaccio of carrots with dates and feta cheese

Serves 4

5 large carrots

2 tablespoons balsamic vinegar

6 tablespoons olive oil

250 g (8 oz) feta cheese

8 dates

3 shallots

salt

Peel the carrots with a swivel-blade vegetable peeler, if you have one.

When peeled, continue to shave each carrot into very thin strips, long or short as you prefer.

Mix together the balsamic vinegar, olive oil and a little salt. Trickle a tablespoonful around each plate.

Dice the feta and pile it in the centre of each plate.

Arrange the carrot strips around the feta. If the strips are long, you could make them into flower shapes or, if short, simply scatter them.

Cut the dates into small pieces and finely chop the shallots. Scatter them over each plate.

Pour the remaining vinaigrette over the carrots or around each plate, if you prefer.

Suggestion

This carpaccio makes a good starter.

Cucumber and mint carpaccio

Serves 4

2 cucumbers

300 g (10 fl oz) natural yogurt

2 cloves garlic, crushed

4 tablespoons olive oil

8 tablespoons lemon juice

3 or 4 mint sprigs, chopped (set aside a few whole leaves to garnish)

salt and freshly ground black pepper

4 ramekins

Peel the cucumbers thinly.

Slice them into long thin strips, stopping before you reach the centre and the seeds. Put the strips into a colander, sprinkle with salt, and allow to drain for around 20 minutes.

Whip the yogurt to obtain a smooth consistency. Add crushed garlic, olive oil, lemon juice to taste, and the chopped mint. Season with salt and pepper to taste.

Put this mixture in the bottom of the ramekins and arrange the cucumber strips on top in circles.

Chill in the refrigerator for 5 minutes.

Before serving, place a few mint leaves on top of each dish.

Suggestion

This carpaccio makes a good starter or a refreshing accompaniment to a curry.

Apple carpaccio with goats' cheese

Serves 4

5 crisp red dessert apples

8 tablespoons lemon juice

50 g (2 oz) pine nuts

2 fresh goats' cheeses

10 tablespoons runny honey

Wash, dry, quarter and core the apples, but do not peel. Cut into thin slices.

Put the slices in a deep plate and pour over the lemon juice to prevent discolouration. Dry-fry the pine nuts in a non-stick pan, stirring constantly.

Cut the goats' cheese into thin slices.

Arrange the apple and cheese slices on 4 plates.

Warm the honey in a saucepan over a low heat, then pour over the apples and cheese. Sprinkle over the pine nuts.

Serve immediately.

Orange and chocolate carpaccio

Serves 4

5 oranges

1 tablespoon orange-flower water

juice of 2 oranges

100 g (3½ oz) best quality dark chocolate

For the honey variation

4 tablespoons runny honey

4 teaspoons olive oil

Peel the oranges, removing as much of the pith as possible, and cut in thin slices. Place in a deep plate.

Mix the orange-flower water with the orange juice and pour over the orange slices. Leave to marinate in the refrigerator for at least 1 hour.

Just before serving, melt the chocolate in a bain-marie or in a bowl set over a pan of barely simmering water.

Arrange the orange slices on 4 plates and pour over the marinade.

Pour over the melted chocolate.

This dessert can be prepared in advance (only the melted chocolate needs to be done at the last minute), which will enhance its flavour.

Variation with honey

When the orange slices have marinated in the orange juice and the orange-flower water, arrange them on each plate, leaving out the juice (you can use this as a refreshing drink).

Pour over each plate a tablespoonful of honey and a teaspoonful of olive oil. Serve immediately.

Grapefruit carpaccio

Serves 4

3 small grapefruit

100 g (3½ oz) light brown soft sugar

1 vanilla pod

1 large handful of redcurrants

For the exotic variation

2 teaspoons rum

50 g (2 oz) pine nuts

2–3 mint sprigs

Peel the grapefruit, removing as much of the pith as possible, and slice into very thin rounds.

Arrange the rounds on each plate.

Sprinkle them with sugar, spreading it evenly to dissolve in the grapefruit juice. Refrigerate the plates for 10 minutes.

When ready to serve, split open the vanilla pod lengthways and scrape out the inside with the tip of a knife to scatter the little seeds over each plate. Add the redcurrants.

Variation with pine nuts and rum

For a more exotic version, sprinkle the grapefruit slices with rum before adding the sugar.

Dry-fry the pine nuts and scatter over the grapefruit, together with a few leaves of fresh mint.

Melon and almond carpaccio

Serves 4

100 g (3½ oz) flaked almonds

2 small melons

4 tablespoons runny honey

1 tablespoon sweet fortified wine (port, sherry) or orange liqueur

4 small rosemary sprigs (or several basil or mint leaves)

For the mozzarella cheese variation

200 g (7 oz) mozzarella

Brown the almonds gently in a pan for several minutes, stirring constantly.

Cut the melons in two and remove the seeds. Remove the skin and slice the fruit very thinly, or cut into dice.

Arrange the slices in a fan shape on 4 plates or divide the diced melon among 4 bowls. Drizzle a tablespoon of honey over the melon. Add several drops of fortified wine or orange liqueur and scatter over the almonds.

Decorate each plate with a rosemary sprig or with a few basil or mint leaves.

Variation with mozzarella cheese

Add thin slices of mozzarella to the melon.

Accessories and equipment supplied by:

Habitat, Le Jacquard Français, Potiron.

Styling: Garlone Bardel

© Marabout 2003

text © Marie-Victoire Garcia.

photographs © Akiko Ida

© Hachette Livre (Hachette Pratique) 2003
This edition published by Hachette Illustrated UK, Octopus Publishing Group Ltd.,
2–4 Heron Quays, London E14 4JP

English translation by JMS Books LLP (email: moseleystrachan@blueyonder.co.uk)
Translation © 2004 Octopus Publishing Group

A CIP catalogue for this book is available from the British Library

ISBN: 1 84430 046 3

Printed by Tien Wah, Singapore